IMAGES
of America

LATAH COUNTY

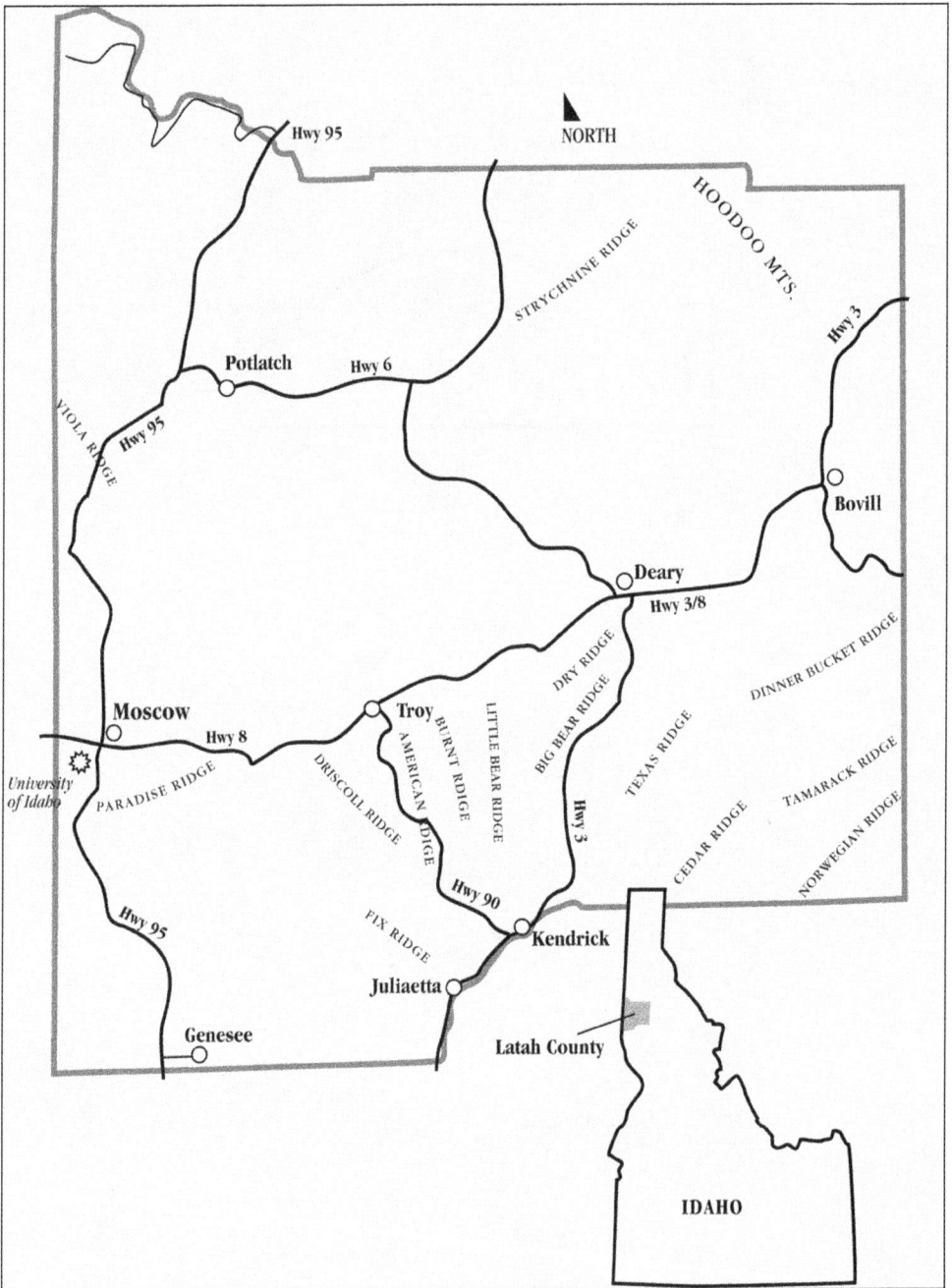

Hwy 95 · NORTH · HOODOO MTS. · STRYCHNINE RIDGE · Hwy 3 · Potlatch · Hwy 6 · VIOLA RIDGE · Hwy 95 · Bovill · Deary · Hwy 3/8 · DRY RIDGE · DINNER BUCKET RIDGE · Moscow · Troy · BIG BEAR RIDGE · LITTLE BEAR RIDGE · BURNT RDIGE · TEXAS RIDGE · Hwy 8 · AMERICAN RIDGE · University of Idaho · PARADISE RIDGE · DRISCOLL RIDGE · Hwy 3 · CEDAR RIDGE · TAMARACK RIDGE · NORWEGIAN RIDGE · Hwy 90 · Hwy 95 · FIX RIDGE · Kendrick · Juliaetta · Latah County · Genesee · IDAHO

Latah County has a current population of nearly 36,000 and is located in the northern Idaho panhandle within a geographically unique region known as the Palouse.

ON THE COVER: Before bulk-storage facilities became commonplace, nearly all grain harvested on the Palouse was sacked and stored in warehouses, like the one in the background of this photograph. This Kendrick warehouse was probably located on the tramway at the east end of town. Tramways were an early solution to the considerable problem of transporting grain from upland farms to boat and train landings situated on rivers below.

IMAGES
of America

LATAH COUNTY

Julie R. Monroe

ARCADIA
PUBLISHING

Published by Arcadia Publishing
Charleston, South Carolina

Library of Congress Catalog Card Number: 2006921675

For all general information contact Arcadia Publishing at:
Telephone 843-853-2070
Fax 843-853-0044
E-mail sales@arcadiapublishing.com
For customer service and orders:
Toll-Free 1-888-313-2665

Visit us on the Internet at www.arcadiapublishing.com

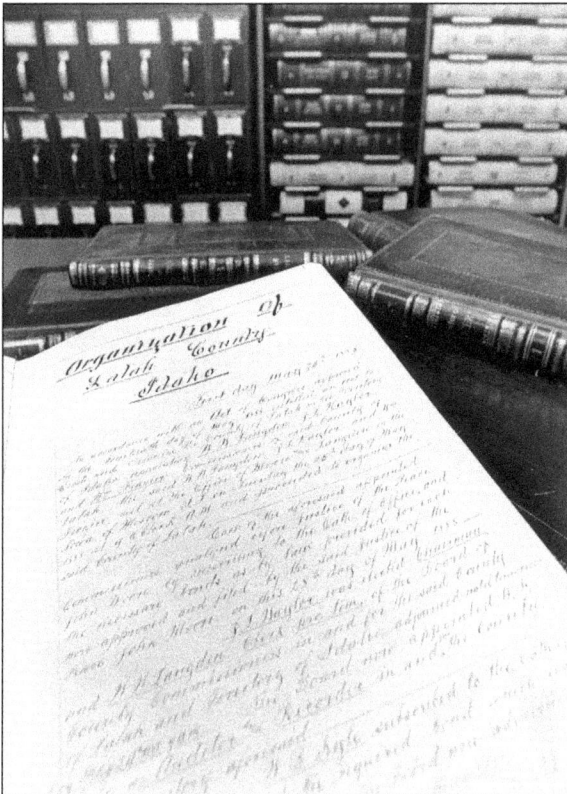

Latah County is the only county in the United States to have been created by an act of Congress. Pres. Grover Cleveland signed the legislation creating the county on May 14, 1888.

CONTENTS

ACKNOWLEDGMENTS

This book would not have been possible without the photographic collection of the Latah County Historical Society, and I am deeply grateful for having had access to this priceless resource. My regard for the individuals—staff and volunteer—who have served and now serve as stewards of our heritage, through their involvement with the historical society, is powerful and abiding.

Because the Latah County Historical Society was the predominant source of photographs for this book, I have provided a photographic credit only when the source was not the historical society. While I have made every attempt to ensure accuracy, I welcome corrections and additional information, particularly relating to the identification of people pictured herein.

Latah County's first officials pose for their official portrait. Pictured, from left to right, are (first row) W. M. Frazier, John Naylor, R. H. Barton, and C. B. Reynolds; (second row) W. W. Landon, John Lieuallen, W. B. Kyle, and Roland Hodgins.

INTRODUCTION

If you want to live in peace, comfort and contentment, unterrified by winds, cyclones, thunder and lightning, sunstroke, blizzards, or cloudbursts, come to Latah County, Idaho. We are exempt from all these things that continually destroy life, property and peace of mind in the East.

—Latah County publicity tract, 1903

Today pride of place is as strong in Latah County as it was in 1903, when the above claim was originally published. Perhaps the reason for such enduring pride is the county's uniqueness as the only one in the United States to have been created by an act of Congress. Or maybe the county's distinctive topography is the explanation. Located within the west-central part of northern Idaho, the northern and eastern parts of Latah County are forested, while the southern and western parts are rolling prairies.

Whatever the reason, the pride beating in the hearts of present-day Latah County citizens is due, in large part, to the remarkable historical legacy left by the county's early citizens. This book pays homage to those early settlers—the residents of Bovill, Deary, Genesee, Moscow, Juliaetta, Kendrick, Potlatch, Troy—and all places in between. It is not a comprehensive history of Latah County, nor was it meant to be. It is one citizen's historical interpretation of the place she now calls home.

The first people to call Latah County home were the Nez Perce, or *Nimiipuu* (Nee-Mee-Poo). A tribe of the Sahaptian language family, the Nez Perce have a rich cultural history, shaped by a deep respect for the land that is as strong today as it was centuries ago when the *Nimiipuu* were the most renowned horsemen of what is now Idaho. Two ancient north/south trails, the Greater Nez Perce Trail and the Red Wolf Trail, passed through what is now Latah County, intersecting about two miles northeast of present-day Moscow.

While the Nez Perce and other native people inhabited the area of Latah County for centuries, it was only around 200 years ago that white men began exploring the area. Like other regions of the American West, the first white men to enter the area were fur trappers. Two decades later, in the 1830s, Christian missionaries appeared, following the trails formed by the very same people they sought to convert. Three decades later, miners arrived and extracted a small fortune in precious metals from the northeastern part of Latah County.

Traditionally trappers, missionaries, and miners seldom put down roots in the areas they explored. But beginning in the 1870s, homesteaders—individuals who wanted nothing else but to settle down—began arriving, attracted by the area's vast fields of grassland and stands of timber. Brothers Asbury and Noah Lieuallen, as well as George W. Tomer, homesteaded in the Moscow area of Latah County in 1871. The village of Genesee was established, about a mile east of the present town, in 1872. In 1878, Rupert Schupfer homesteaded where Juliaetta is now located. Thomas Kirby founded Kendrick in 1889. Homesteader Francis Warren settled the area now known as Bovill, so named in 1899 after the English lord who later built a hotel there. The settlement that would become Troy was incorporated as Vollmer in 1892. In 1905, the Potlatch

Lumber Company began constructing not only the largest white pine sawmill in the world but also the town that would bear the company's name. Two years later, the town of Deary, named after then Potlatch Lumber Company general manager William Deary, was created.

Present-day Latah County was once part of Nez Perce County. Disgruntled with the inconvenience of traveling to the county seat in Lewiston, which was over 60 miles away from Moscow and at an elevation 2,000 feet less, early residents soon began campaigning for their own county. Defeated at the territorial level, the populace took their fight to the nation's capital. Through the efforts of Idaho's delegate in Congress and a senator from Oregon, Congress passed the legislation creating Latah County. On May 14, 1888, Pres. Grover Cleveland signed the bill into law.

A committee of residents, led by William J. McConnell, who would go on to become the state of Idaho's third governor, created the new county's name by blending two Nimiipuu words: *La-Koh*, meaning "white pine trees," and *Tah-ol*, the term for the stone pestles the Nimiipuu used to grind camas roots. Thus, for McConnell and the county's other early citizens, Latah meant "the place of pine and pestle," a reference to the county's contrasting stands of timber and fields of grass. Today there is no camas to harvest and the white pine is less plentiful, but for most Latah County citizens, there is pride that for them Latah County is a place that means home.

From her position at center stage, Miss Genesee appears to have won the title for which the other Latah County beauty queens were competing, probably sometime in the late 1950s. Behind her, from left to right, are Miss Troy, Miss Moscow, Miss Potlatch, Miss ?, and Miss Kendrick.

One

BOVILL AND DEARY

Amidst the forests of east-central Latah County are the communities of Bovill and Deary, their histories linked by the fortunes of the Potlatch Lumber Company. Bovill was known as Warren Meadows until a visiting English lord, Hugh Bovill, bought the homestead of Francis Warren in 1899. Returning from England with his wife and daughters in 1901, Bovill set about fulfilling his dream of developing Bovill as a resort. In 1910, however, the Bovill family left the area, accepting that their vision for the community was incompatible with that of the Potlatch Lumber Company, which had begun harvesting timber from the area three years earlier.

Although settled as early as the 1880s and 1890s primarily by Scandinavians from the Midwest, the town of Deary was not platted until 1907. In 1905, the Potlatch Lumber Company decided to build a Washington, Idaho & Montana Railway station at the site of present-day Deary. The town that grew up around the depot was named in honor of William Deary, who, as general manager of the Potlatch Lumber Company, directed the construction of the town and the lumber mill.

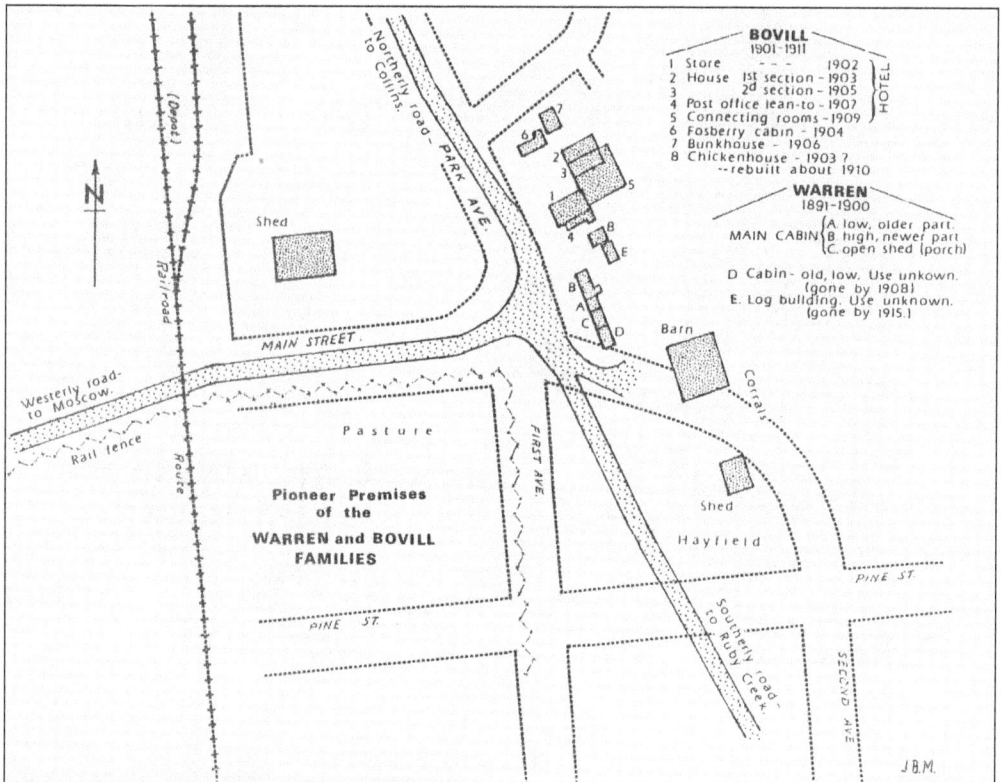

John B. Miller, one of Latah County's most prolific amateur historians, used historical photographs to construct this map of the "Pioneer Premises of the Warren and Bovill Families." Francis Warren homesteaded the area of the present town of Bovill around 1890. In 1901, he sold his property to Englishman Hugh Bovill.

Hugh Bovill, the youngest son of Sir William Bovill, left his native England in search of opportunities in places as far-flung as Ceylon and Latah County. With wife Charlotte, Bovill built the Hotel Bovill to accommodate vacationers seeking a pristine wilderness hideaway or those hoping to take advantage of the area's fine hunting and fishing.

As this interior view reveals, the Hotel Bovill was a place of elegance in the wilderness. By 1910, the hotel had been expanded three times, the last to house Potlatch Lumber Company officials. Shortly after Bovill's incorporation in 1907, the Potlatch Lumber Company began purchasing the land surrounding the resort.

One of Bovill's early businesses was E. K. Parker's general store. No newcomer to Latah County, Parker had mined gold in the Hoodoo Mining District east of Potlatch and operated a store in Princeton before moving to Bovill in 1908.

An early Bovill business was Peter Johnson's mercantile store. Johnson is the man on the right of the building's entrance and on the left is his son Hjalmer. The date of the photograph is unknown, but it is probably from the early 1900s.

Around 1907, the Potlatch Lumber Company established 14 logging camps in the area surrounding Bovill. Predictably, saloons and bawdy houses soon followed. This 1909 letter from the company's assistant manager Allison Laird reveals just how determined company officials were to keep their workforce sober.

The Washington, Idaho & Montana Railway, owned and operated by the Potlatch Lumber Company, reached Bovill in 1907. Pictured here is Bovill's depot that same year. From Bovill, the track ran to Palouse, Washington, where it connected with the Northern Pacific line.

The Potlatch Lumber Company took over the hospital built by the Chicago, Milwaukee & Puget Sound Railroad in 1910. According to historian Keith C. Petersen, the Bovill Hospital was operated "under contract with the Western Hospital Association of Seattle in exchange for the mandatory one dollar per fee that Potlatch received from its workers."

Veterinary surgeon and dentist George Palmer, according to the sign on his barn, specialized in teeth and feet. According to the inscription on the back of the photograph, the Bovill veterinarian also "doctored" people.

Over a century ago, draft horses were a part of almost all logging operations. Common breeds were the Percheron, Clydesdale, Shire, and Belgian. This photograph was taken in 1908 near Bovill; the Potlatch Lumber Company probably owned the horses.

An early Bovill-area business was the Cedar View Dairy, located on the farm of William and Minnie Miller, one-half mile south of Bovill. Minnie Miller is in this 1915 photograph with her children, daughter Luzelle and son John. John went on to write *The Trees Grew Tall*, an account of Bovill's early years. (Keno is the dog in Luzelle's lap.)

This photograph of Bovill's Main Street was probably taken in 1917 or 1918. Pictured, from left to right, are Delia Crawford (Bovill's druggist), Mrs. Dave Ellison (her husband owned Bovill's Spokane Hotel), Mrs. Charles White, Mrs. Carlton Stockwell, and Mrs. R. T. Witty (whose husband was a dentist).

These men were photographed in the Bovill Recreation Hall that was managed by the Potlatch Lumber Company. Pictured, from left to right, are Oscar Hagbom, Loren Ireland, Milford Welch, Andrew Sversted, Earl Ritzheimer, Julius Crane, Bill Steele, Chet Yangel, Clarence Haag, John Kelly, Thomas Femreite, John Zagelou, Ray Bonner, Delbert Byers, and Irwin Fisher.

BOVILL, IDAHO

Very few towns the size of Bovill can boast of as many advantages and so many industries. Lack of space prevents us from saying as much as we would like to do, but we give the following data:

E. K. Parker .... General Merchandise

W. M. Watt .... Pool Hall and Restaurant

M. Hilton .... Barber Shop

R. T. Witty .... Dentist

Dave Ellison .... Spokane Hotel

D. Crawford .... Drug Store

V. See .... Dry Goods

First State Bank .... S. H. Crotinger, Cashier

R. W. Chambers .... Shoe Repair Shop

John Groh & Co. .... General Merchandise

J. A. Anderson .... General Merchandise

W. B. Pollock .... Garage

Elizabeth David .... Boarding House

L. Denevan .... Picture Show

Green Chambers .... Rooming House

Dr. F. C. Gibson .... Bovill Hospital

S. R. Byerly .... Lumber Yard

George St. Germain .... Dray

During its heyday, Bovill was the third largest town in Latah County, behind Moscow and Potlatch. This page from the May 1921 Bovill High School annual is a listing of just a few of the town's businesses. By the 1930s, the area's prime timber was gone, as was Bovill's economic vitality.

Prior to 1927, a town-owned, steam-driven plant provided Bovill's electricity. In 1927, local men were hired to build a 22,000-volt transmission line through Deary and Bovill and rebuild the lines in the town. Among the crew were the men in this photograph who, from left to right, are Herman Schupfer, Tony Eichner, Axel Burkland, Roy Wells, and Fred Fonholtz.

Atop the 80-foot pole in this photograph, dated 1928, are Herman Schupfer and Phil Johns. In 1927, regional utility Washington Water Power bought and completed the electrical line running from Troy to Deary and Bovill that had been started by the Potlatch Consolidated Electric Company.

Among the members of Bovill's 1904 girls' basketball team is the daughter of Hugh and Charlotte Bovill. Pictured, from left to right, are Clara Stockwell, Althea Adair, Nellie Woods, Mabel Smith, Mattie Stockwell, Florence Smith, and Dorothy Bovill. The little girl in front is Edna Woods.

Members of the 1933 eighth-grade class at Bovill Grade School pose for Spokane photographer Leo Oestreicher. Many of Oestreicher's black and white photographs were made into color postcards and sold as souvenirs.

May Day festivities were once an important part of American community life, and no celebration was complete without the selection of a queen. The 1933 May Queen of Bovill Grade School is pictured here with her rather extended court.

Spokane photographer Leo Oestreicher, who specialized in photographing school groups, took this one of the Bovill High School football team in 1936.

Perhaps Spokane, Washington, photographer Leo Oestreicher was reminded of the Three Graces, the Greek goddesses of joy, charm, and beauty, when he took this photograph of a trio of Bovill High School coeds sometime in the mid-1930s.

While the town of Deary was not created until 1907, its vicinity had been settled as early as the 1880s and 1890s. Many of the homesteaders, such as the Bjorkland and Bjerke families, were Scandinavians who left the Midwest behind to establish farms and sawmills on timbered land.

All that is known about this trio of siblings, Gus, Annie, and Ed Swenson, is that they were from the Deary area.

Joe and Lou Wells, along with their children, left North Carolina to settle in the Deary area in 1889. Joe soon became a successful lumberman and farmer, and Lou garnered a well-deserved reputation as an excellent cook. This photograph was probably taken in the 1890s.

Although he never lived there, the town of Deary was named for William Deary, the general manager of the Potlatch Lumber Company. In 1905, Deary selected the present site of Deary as the site of a station for his company's railroad. During the next two years, Deary established the Deary Townsite Company to sell land he secured after it had been cleared of timber.

After the sale of town lots began on September 24, 1907, Deary grew quickly. Listed in a 1908 Polk's Business Directory are several general stores, as well as the Carlson Hotel, a dairy, two sawmills, a drugstore, a harness shop, a doctor's office, a barbershop, and a livery stable.

After opening a studio on July 16, 1909, photographer Anton Lee documented Deary goings-on for many years. Lee's studio was located in the upper part of his home in the background of this photograph. While the men in this image are unidentified, it seems clear they wished to be pictured with hunting, fishing, and prospecting accoutrements. Note the dog sitting on the stump between the two men at right.

This portrait of John A. Thomas, at left, was taken in Deary in 1916 (perhaps by Deary photographer Anton Lee). The identity of the young man at right is unknown, but he may have been one of John's brothers—Sidney, Dewey, or Fernando.

The inscription on the back of this photograph of Della Blalock explains her distinctive apparel. Appearing as a "Daughter of the West," Blalock won a costume competition with the homemade outfit she is wearing. She may have been the daughter of one of Deary's early settlers, Joe Blalock, who later sold his property to the Potlatch Lumber Company.

Sadly, neither the date of this photograph nor the identities of the members of the Deary Cornet Band is known.

These members of the 1933 Deary High School basketball team, pictured, from left to right, are (first row) coach Huddleson, Boyd Beckett, Darrell Waide, Carl Nelson, and Louis Contos; (second row) Bob Morton, Walt Mallery, Norman Nelson, Billy King, and Howard Parks. A verse from the 1925 Deary Fight Song reads, "You'll find us ready and steady boosting for Deary High."

Pictured here is the general store of William S. Miller, which was located in the once thriving community of Helmer, four miles east of Deary. The community was named for Potlatch Lumber Company timber cruiser William Helmer. Miller and his wife Minnie are in the back row at left.

This photograph of a Potlatch Lumber Company logging-camp dining area probably was taken at Camp 6. Started in 1907 and first located about one mile north of Helmer, Camp 6 was the headquarters for sleigh logging, in which horses pulled sleighs from the forests in the park area of Latah County to the bottom of the canyon on Potlatch Creek.

Two

GENESEE

Located in the southwestern part of Latah County, Genesee is nestled within some of the most fertile farmland in the Palouse. One theory about how Genesee got its name is that one of the first men to explore the area noticed how closely it resembled his former home, the Genesee Valley in New York state. Another is that Genesee is a variation of the word "Genesis."

By 1872, "Old Genesee," a small settlement about one mile east of Genesee's present site, had developed. "New" Genesee came about in 1886 when John P. Vollmer, an agent of the Spokane and Palouse Railway, and Jacob Rosenstein, owner of the "Old" Genesee town site, could not agree on a price for the railroad's right-of-way. In response, Vollmer stopped the track one mile west of the original town, built a terminus, and began acquiring acreage around it. Soon businesspeople, including Rosenstein, began moving to Vollmer's town site, and on October 23, 1889, the new town was incorporated.

This drawing of the H. B. Hodgins place in Genesee was done by T. E. Miller and presented on April 4, 1886. The vast stretches of farmland, covered with bunch grass, wildflowers, and thorn bushes, attracted settlers to the Genesee area, and this drawing preserves a representative example of an early farmstead.

Thomas Tierney was one of the earliest settlers in Latah County. A native of Ireland, Tierney settled west of Genesee in an area called Thorncreek in September 1870. Initially he grew wheat one year and flax the next, but while the blue fields of flax were a sight to behold, wheat eventually became the dominant crop. Tierney died in Moscow at the age of 94.

Arriving in 1871, Jacob Kambitsch, a native of Austria, was one of the first homesteaders in the Genesee Valley. A soldier of the Union Army, he is pictured here in his Civil War uniform. (The author lives in the Moscow home built in 1935 by Jacob's daughter Sophie and her husband, William Marineau.)

Successful, but unpopular, businessman John P. Vollmer opened a general store and a bank in Genesee, housing it in the building in this photograph. The facade of the second story, erected in 1892, was a prefabricated storefront. The structure is in the National Register of Historic Places.

Bee Hive Store

Genesee, Idaho

This Ticket entitles you to one chance on

Wellington Piano

To be given away January 30, 1906. Every 50 cent purchase entitles you to a ticket.

GEO. H. HOBSON.

☞ KEEP THIS TICKET.

After its sale to George H. Hobson, the Genesee Mercantile Company became the Bee Hive Store. It was housed in the Alexander Building that was constructed in 1896 by Joseph Alexander, a businessman with interests in several towns, including Kendrick, Juliaetta, and Lewiston.

The man in this 1890s photograph could be Leon Follett, who with brother John, opened a general store in Genesee on Fir Street around 1895. In 1898, the brothers constructed a brick building to house their store. Their nephew Mahlon eventually bought into the business and operated it for nearly 50 years.

Matt Kambitsch, behind the bar, operated the Genesee Brewery with Joseph Geiger beginning in 1889; the brewery also featured a saloon in the front of the building facing Chestnut Street. In 1902, Geiger became sole owner of the brewery and, by 1908, it was producing bottled beer. The customers in this photograph are, from left to right, Amos Kern, John Nelson, and Jim Dutton.

The Commercial Cream Company is listed among many Genesee businesses in a c. 1910 newspaper. Charles Geltz is the driver, but the identities of the other men are unknown.

HEROES OF MANILA — CALOOCAN — GUADALUPE.

WELCOME

Memorial Arch, Gen

Printed for W. J. Herman, Pub

ME.

HEROES.
OF.
MANILA
LAGUNA DE BAY.
SANTA CRUZ

Idaho.

ier. Genesee, Idaho.

The people of Genesee constructed the arch in this photograph and staged a parade to welcome home area veterans of the 1898 Spanish-American War. A Genesee post of the American Legion was formed following World War I and named in honor of Henry Bielenberg and John Schooler, who were killed in action during that war.

The individuals in this photograph of an early Genesee butcher shop are, from left to right, Dan Healy, Carl Nelson, Milton Roder, Frank Harris Jr, and Frank Harris Sr.

The date of this panorama of early Genesee is unknown. While its main thoroughfare is unpaved, the community appears to have electrical service if the electrical poles are any indication. As early as the first decade of the 20th century, Washington Water Power had built a high-voltage transmission line to Genesee.

Genesee Valley Lutheran Church, pictured here in this painting by Latah County artist Alf Dunn, is the oldest and first organized Lutheran Congregation in Idaho. On March 17, 1878, the first service was conducted and a congregation was formally organized as Our Savior's Lutheran Church. The building in this painting was constructed in 1911 and is on the National Register of Historic Places.

Pictured here is the interior of Genesee's early Catholic church, St. Mary's. Beginning in 1896, the parish operated a parochial school, St. Joseph's, which was staffed by Benedictine sisters. The original church, dedicated in 1890, was destroyed by fire in 1961. A new St. Mary's was completed in 1965.

Public education in Genesee goes back to the establishment of the first school in 1879. This class photograph shows the members of Genesee's sixth and seventh grades in 1908. Pictured, from left to right, are (first row) Chet Gage, Louis Mochel, Milton Rader, Carl Flomer, Clarence Flomer, Steven Kambitsch, Mahlon Follett, and Clarence Trail; (second row) Clarence Peterson, unidentified, Louis Steltz, Gretchan Smith, Ilah Larrabee, Myrtle Swenson, and Adeline Broppler; (third row) Norma Jackson, unidentified, unidentified, Faythe Follett, unidentified, teacher Mary Wardrobe, Ella Nebelsieck, Marie Bumyass, and Julie Kane.

The undefeated 1911–1912 Genesee High School basketball team was a regional champion. Pictured, from left to right, are (first row) Charles Gray, James Keane, and Melvin Wardrobe; (second row) Andrew Wardrobe, manager Herbert Martinson, and John Wardrobe.

Leo Oestreicher of Spokane, Washington, took this photograph of Genesee's third and fourth grades in 1934 or 1935. From the late 1920s to around 1945, Oestreicher traveled the region taking a variety of photographs, particularly of school groups.

According to the inscription on the back of this c. 1910 photograph, the leader of this Boy Scout troop is Walter Casebolt. The author, however, wonders if the leader actually might be Walter's brother Victor, who served on the board of the Inland Empire Council of the Boy Scouts of America for many years.

On March 17, 1908, the Farmers' Educational and Cooperative Union of America, a national marketing organization, granted a group of Genesee farmers a charter to form the Genesee Union No. 4. One of the first tasks the group undertook was the construction of a 60,000-bushel sack warehouse on the west end of Genesee. This photograph is from around 1909.

Geneseeans seems to be bearing the snowy winter of 1912–1913 with good cheer. The identities of the people in this photograph are unknown.

Like saloons, pool halls were once fixtures of community social life. Nate Edwards, third from the left, established the Pastime Pool Hall in 1913. The other men in this photograph are unidentified.

Genesee was no exception to the women's clubs movement that swept the nation during the last decades of the 19th century. In this *c.* 1910 image, members of the Monday Bunch gather for a costume party. The inscription on the photograph provides only the last names of the women, which from left to right, are Mrs. Jain, Mrs. Hanson, Mrs. Nelson, Mrs. Follett, Mrs. Carlan, Mrs. Herman, Mrs. Shork, Mrs. Casebolt, and Mrs. Smith.

From 1945 to 1975, Ronald "Stub" Geltz and his wife, Jerry, operated the Pastime Pool Hall, leasing the building from Stub's uncle, Ray Edwards. According to a centennial history of Genesee, Stub was "known far and wide for his good hamburgers and droll sense of humor."

A still important element of Genesee's community life is Community Day, which started out as the Genesee Horse Show. From the early 1900s to the 1930s, the three-day Genesee Horse Show drew people from throughout the region, including members of the Nez Perce tribe, pictured here in 1916.

Genesee's Community Day is celebrated with a number of festivities, including games, meals, dances, and parades. Perhaps the little girls in this 1935 photograph labeled, "Community Day in Genesee, Ida," participated in the 1935 Community Day parade.

With its large Norwegian population, it is no surprise that Norwegian Independence Day on May 17 was celebrated for many years in the Genesee area. This photograph captures the 1904 festivities held at the Tweedt Farm. According to the *Genesee News*, a crowd of nearly 1,000 people celebrated the holiday with speeches, music, and games.

In 1885, John and Mary Lorang moved to Genesee from Wisconsin and eventually named their 160-acre farm White Spring Ranch in honor of a nearby water source. The couple poses in 1901 in front of their home with their children. Pictured, from left to right, are Mollie, Peter, Bertha, Mary (sitting), Albert, Viola, Bernard, John, Charles (sitting), Henry, Christine, and Martha.

The Spurbeck family was one of the earliest to settle in the Genesee area. The family of Emma and Charles Spurbeck, pictured here around 1900, from left to right, are (first row) Emma, Marguerite, and Charles; and (second row) David, Winnie, Charles Rollin, Ethel, Lloyd, and Pearl. The December 12, 1902, entry from the journal of Charles Rollin states, "Fair. Snow. I took my first music lesson this winter on the organ tonight. I swept the church after school."

Benjamin and Lewis Jain, pictured here in 1904, were the sons of Walter and Lela Jain. At the time of his death in 1984, Ben Jain was one of the oldest working cowboys in north central Idaho. His father's family was one of the first to settle in the Genesee area, arriving in 1878.

Mr. and Mrs. Raleigh Hampton are pictured here with their daughter Marie in 1939. Until her death in 1996, Marie was the unofficial historian of Genesee. She married Donald F. (Dick) Scharnhorst on November 15, 1947, in Genesee, and the couple had three sons, Robert, James, and Bruce.

Three

JULIAETTA
AND KENDRICK

Situated in the valley of the Potlatch River, Juliaetta and Kendrick enjoy such a mild climate that the rich agricultural region in which the two communities are located is known as the "banana belt" of Latah County. Homesteaded as early as 1878 by Rupert Schupfer, Juliaetta was first known as Schupfer or Schuperville. Another early homesteader, Charles Snyder, established a post office in 1881 and named it Juliaetta in honor of his two daughters, Julia and Etta. In 1890, Schupfer became Juliaetta after residents requested the name be changed to match that of the post office.

Thomas Kirby established Kendrick as Latah in 1888. Citizens agreed to change the name to Kendrick when the Northern Pacific Railroad promised to extend a line to the community when James P. Kendrick was the chief engineer of the railroad company. Resiliency marks the history of Kendrick and its residents as the community was flooded in 1900 and burned twice, first in 1902 and then again in 1904.

Rupert Schupfer and his brother Mathias settled in the Juliaetta area in the 1870s. The people in this photograph probably are Rupert and Constania Schupfer and one of their children, perhaps son Henry. Mathias and his wife, Aloisia, a native Austrian as were the Schupfer brothers, had three children, Otto, Herman, and Ida, born on their homestead north of Juliaetta.

During the 1890s, Juliaetta was the "end of the line" for the Northern Pacific's run south from Spokane, Washington, to Lewiston, Idaho, and as many as four separate passenger trains arrived in town daily. Perhaps some of the individuals in this photograph of the Valley Hotel, taken before 1900, were passengers on their way to Lewiston.

Juliaetta, pictured here in 1908, experienced a commercial boom beginning in 1903 when Robert Foster established the Foster School of Healing. Goods were available from a variety of stores as were the services of a barber, dentist, pharmacist, attorney, and undertaker. With their leisure time, residents could visit the ice-cream parlor, the roller-skating rink, the movie theater, or the pool hall.

Robert Foster, pictured here with his family, founded of one of Juliaetta's most unique businesses, the Foster School of Healing. Foster treated thousands of people suffering from a variety of diseases, especially skin cancer, by offering them a treatment of nutritional, osteopathic, and suggestive therapeutics. He also trained others in his techniques.

In 1902, a private home built before the turn of the 20th century became the Palace Hotel that was operated by Benjamin Taylor and Frank Fox. Perhaps some of the visitors in this c. 1904 photograph were visiting Juliaetta to be treated at the Foster School of Healing.

In the early 1900s, Abram A. Adams built the home in this photograph. Known as "the castle," this structure, now a privately owned museum, was constructed of concrete blocks with partitions of concrete several inches thick.

The Juliaetta Mercantile Company, pictured here around 1910, was also known as Alexander's Store. Joseph Alexander Jr., whose father constructed store buildings in both Kendrick and Genesee, managed the store.

TURN OVER A NEW LEAF

THE NEW LEAF
Resolved that this year I will put some money into the Bank for safety and in case of necessity

THE OLD LEAF

1912 January 1912
S. M. T. W. T. F. S.
1 2 3 4 5 6
7 8 9 10 11 12 13
14 15 16 17 18 19 20
21 22 23 24 25 26 27
28 29 30 31

People find sudden fortunes less often than they find "four-leaf" clover. Don't wait for good luck to strike you. But MAKE your luck BY REGULARLY SAVING a part of your income.

Make OUR Bank YOUR Bank.

Capital $10,000.00
Responsibility $65,000.00
Established 1900
E. W. PORTER, Cashier

BANK OF JULIAETTA,
Juliaetta, Idaho

In its heyday, Juliaetta had two banks. In addition to the Bank of Juliaetta, there was also the Citizens' State Bank, which existed only through 1913.

With their team, Mr. Taylor, Mr. Biddison, and an unidentified gentlemen grade the streets of Juliaetta. This photograph was probably taken around 1910, the year that Robert Foster moved his practice from Juliaetta to Clarkston, Washington.

The inscription on the back of this *c.* 1915 photograph of workers at Juliaetta's cannery identifies some, but not all of the workers. Pictured, from left to right, are (first row) unidentified, Crystal Ottosen, Buchanan, Louise Wright, Mr. and Mrs. Mahon, and Kathryn; (second row) Keefer, Smith, McGlynn, Lulu Buchanan, Mrs. Harry Wright, John Kite, Otto Schupfer, Lillian Ottosen, McGlynn, Mona Rheams, Ida Schupfer, Ida Aldrich, Ella Brummons, and Mrs. Brummons.

The mild climate of the Potlatch River Valley made farming a lucrative industry in Juliaetta's early days, and a variety of grain, vegetable, and fruit crops were grown. The gentlemen in this photograph are harvesting potatoes. Note the tramway leading to the warehouse in the background.

Rail trams were how farmers ingeniously solved the problem of moving crops from the fields to transportation landings. The Juliaetta rail tram in this *c.* 1912 photograph was Latah County's largest and was built by grain dealers Lawrence and Porter in the 1890s at a cost of $25,000.

Arthur Perryman and Herman Schupfer are perched on a rail tramcar around 1912. Herman, with his brother Otto, operated the tramway that ran from a Juliaetta warehouse to the top of Potlatch Ridge. Arthur, a native of Juliaetta, later operated a grocery store.

Members of Juliaetta's baseball team strike a brotherly pose around 1914. Perhaps because it was the only organized sport then available, amateur baseball was exceedingly popular during the 1880s and 1890s. Even small towns could have more than one team, and rivalries between neighboring communities were common.

This c. 1900 "birds-eye view" of Kendrick clearly reveals the community's low elevation in the valley of the Potlatch River, which was a setting perfect for growing prize-winning fruit. In 1893, Kendrick fruit grower John Hepler was recognized for the most perfect apples on display at the Chicago World's Fair.

The exhibit pictured here was displayed at the Potlatch Fruit Fair held in Kendrick in 1896. A 1903 agricultural summary indicating crop distribution reveals the significance of agriculture to the early history of the area: wheat at 28,000 acres; barley and oats at 5,000 acres each; corn and beans at 1,000 acres; apples at 3,315 acres; prunes at 684 acres; and grapes at 72 acres.

Members of the Burns, Wilson, and Metcalf families pose for the camera while making molasses on the Scottie Wilson homestead near Kendrick in 1894. Pictured, from left to right, are Donald Burns, Mary Burns Wilson, Kate Burns Metcalf, John Burns, three unidentified people, Carson Metcalf, Grover Metcalf, and an unidentified man.

On December 15, 1899, a train loaded with steel rails went out of control in Kendrick and plunged into the Potlatch River. In early January, melting snow and rain flooded the river, which was partially dammed by the debris from the train wreck. Under the pressure, the fill supporting the railroad bed gave way and water rushed into the streets of Kendrick.

On January 10, 1900, a devastating flood struck Kendrick, taking lives and destroying businesses and residences. Despite the catastrophe, someone found the time to take this photograph of the floodwaters in front of the St. Elmo Hotel in Kendrick.

This photograph of the aftermath of the fire that started on the sawdust floor of Kendrick's Pacific Hotel on Friday, August 5, 1904, reveals the complete destruction it caused. Financial damage resulting from the fire was estimated at $300,000.

Kendrick High School students pose here with J. P. Barackman, then superintendent of schools, around 1904. Pictured, from left to right, are (first row) Nona Benscoter; (second row) Elsie Keene and Georgia Wright (third row) Mabel Benscoter, Barackman, and Georgia Hupp; (fourth row) Belva Gooding, Eddie Atchison, Babe Davidson, Bill Greene, and Elva Roberts. The Benscoter girls were cousins.

Photographer Leo Oestreicher from Spokane, Washington, took this image of Kendrick High School's class of 1936. From the late 1920s to about 1945, Oestreicher traveled the region photographing a variety of subjects, particularly school groups, sports, and other activities for school annuals.

Leo Oestreicher took this image of members of the Kendrick High School chapter of the Future Farmers of America (FFA) in the mid-1930s. The Latah County Historical Society has preserved many of the photographs Oestricher took of Latah County school groups in the mid-1930s, but this is the only one of an FFA chapter.

Members of the Kendrick High School band pose for their photograph around 1939.

Big Bear Ridge farmer Amos Moore married Julia Ingle on July 24, 1893. Julia came west with her parents, David and Maria, and brothers Henry Leon and King David in 1884. King is pictured here in June 1909 on his honeymoon with wife Florence Linnie Hupp, who grew up on Little Bear Ridge. The couple had four children: Gerald, William, Alcie, and Betty.

Alexander and Kate Galloway arrived in Latah County in 1898 and eventually settled on Big Bear Ridge. Alexander is at the wheel of his 1914 Ford, one of the first automobiles in the area. With him in front are sons John (center) and Henry and in back are wife Kate and daughters Annie and Mary.

Four

MOSCOW

The Nez Perce, the area's earliest inhabitants, called what is now Moscow *Tat-kin-mah*, or "place of the spotted deer." Not only was Moscow special for its abundant fields of the essential camas, it was also where mule deer and their spotted young summered. Located in southwestern Latah County, Moscow was first unofficially known as Hog Heaven and then Paradise Valley when it was granted its first post office. It is likely that Samuel Neff, an early homesteader, chose the name Moscow after his birthplace in Moscow, Pennsylvania, when he was filling out post-office application papers.

Brothers Asbury and Noah Lieuallen are most often credited with founding Moscow upon their arrival in 1871. With their help and that of other homesteaders, Moscow developed as a supply and trade center. It became the county seat in 1888 and was selected as the site of the University of Idaho in 1889. Today Moscow's population is a little less than 22,000.

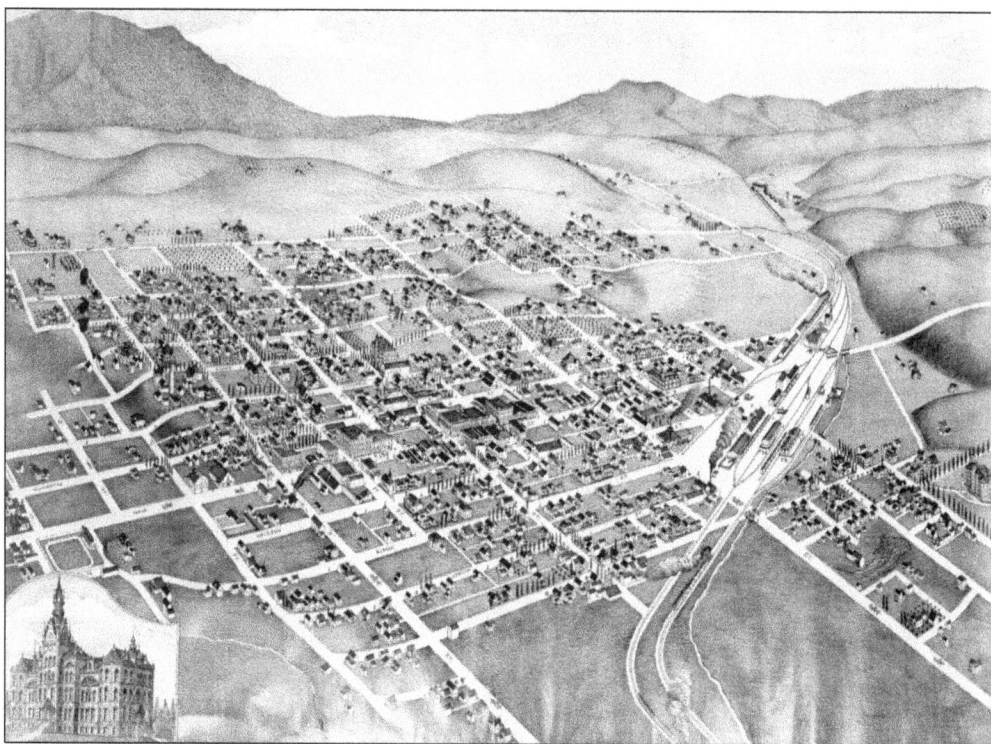

Famed cartographer Augustus Koch drew this 1897 *Bird's Eye View of the City of Moscow, Latah County, Idaho.* Before photography became accessible, panoramic maps were a popular way of depicting towns and cities. Koch, a native of Germany who served in the Union army during the Civil War, was well regarded for the detail and accuracy of his maps.

Henry Erichson, a landscape and portrait artist, took this photograph of Angie Scully in Moscow when Idaho was still a territory. No information is available about Miss Scully, but Erichson, who arrived in Moscow in 1884, would go on to become the community's premier photographer. In 1906, he left Moscow but stayed in Latah County, moving to Driscoll Ridge near Troy.

The claims of four of Moscow's earliest permanent settlers met at the current intersection of Sixth and Main Streets. Probably in 1876, Almon Asbury Lieuallen, James Deakin, Henry McGregor, and John Russell, pictured here with his wife Margaret, donated 30 acres of their land as the basis for a commercial district, a city center.

Thyrza McGregor, at far right, was the wife of Henry McGregor, one of the four settlers who donated land to form Moscow's commercial center. A widow when she and her children, mother, and brother moved to Moscow in 1877, Thyrza married Henry McGregor in 1879.

Almon Asbury Lieuallen is pictured here with wife Sarah and their children John, Lillie, and Burton. Almon and Sarah were married in Lewiston, Idaho, on July 4, 1871. The couple's first child, Mary Ann, was born in the spring of 1872 but died at age five. Lillie was born in 1874, John in 1877, and Burton in 1880.

Lillian Woodworth Otness was the daughter of Lillie Lieuallen Woodworth. Mrs. Otness' father, Jay Woodworth, married Lillie Irene Lieuallen in 1893 in the Lieuallen family home on Moscow's Almon Street.

One of Lillie Lieuallen Woodworth's closest friends was Bertie Gritman, pictured here with her husband Charles sometime in the 1930s. Dr. and Mrs. Gritman, along with Dr. R. C. Coffey, established Latah County's first hospital when they converted the McGregor House into a medical facility in 1897.

Dr. J. G. Wilson Family

Prior to his death in 1933, Dr. Charles Gritman purchased a fine home in Moscow's most prestigious neighborhood, the Fort Russell District. In the 1940s, the home was sold to another physician, J. G. Wilson. The extended Wilson family offers its Season's Greetings here sometime in the late 1960s.

Frank B. Robinson, in the fur coat at far left, is pictured distributing refreshments to Civilian Conservation Corps workers on land he donated to Latah County for a public park. Robinson founded Psychiana, the world's first mail-order religion in Moscow in 1929.

Mattie Headington, at left, was a Moscow teacher who went on to serve as superintendent of schools. The woman at right is identified as Miss Aauch, but nothing else is known about her. This photograph is from around 1900.

Mattie Headington is pictured here with husband William and daughter Sarah Grace. The date of this photograph is unidentified, but it is known that Sarah, born in 1893, died on February 13, 1900. Following a career as an educator, Mr. Headington was admitted to the bar in 1898, but he died on April 25, 1899.

One of Moscow's early teachers was Frances "Fanny" Reeder Coats, pictured here with her family. She married H. L. Coats on January 15, 1891. Mrs. Coats probably died in 1901, and interestingly her obituary indicates that she was survived by her husband and her niece but does not mention any children.

Gottfried "George" Weber, posing in the 1890s with wife Kate, bought the house built by Dr. James W. Reeder, father of Frances Coats. Weber, a native of Germany, was the premier harness maker on the Palouse and was also active in civic affairs.

In addition to participating in Moscow city government, "George" Weber also served as chief of Moscow's volunteer fire department. He is the seated gentleman with the white cap, and leaning against him is his son John. The appliqués on the mens' shirts indicate that they were members of the Capitol Hose Company No. 1.

This photograph was taken in the late 1950s at the ceremony honoring John C. Muerman, Moscow's first superintendent of schools. Conspicuous among the attendees are two Ursuline nuns at far right who were teachers at St. Mary's School, which was founded in 1908 as the Ursuline Academy.

In 1969, members of the first grade of West Park Elementary School pose for their class photograph. One of their teachers was Florence Cline, pictured at far right.

"Kelly" Cline, at far right, the husband of schoolteacher Florence Cline, is pictured here with his 1951 bowling buddies Carl Smith, "Doc" Baker, Tom Aaring, and Oscar Nelson. According to the photograph, the total age of these champion bowlers was 305 years.

According to the inscription on the back of the photograph, the 1917 Moscow High School girl's basketball team was a "good one." Pictured, from left to right, are Flora Loomis, Olive Frazier, Ruth Burton, Ruth Harris, Pearl Buchan, and Mabel Drury.

Not all of the participants in the 1911 Fourth of July "girl's race" are identified, but among those competing are sisters Annette and Margaret McCallie and Julia Moore, daughter of Charles and Julia A. Moore. Annette and Margaret were the daughters of James McCallie, a dentist, and Margaret would go on to marry Julia's brother, Fred Moore.

Sometime in the 1920s, a group of Moscow Camp Fire Girls poses for its photograph. Pictured, from left to right, are (first row) Marjorie Woodward, Betty Horton, Esther Fitch, Edna Scott, and Bonnie Woodward (Marjorie's sister); (second row) Mary Axtell and an unidentified girl (perhaps Elizabeth Vincent); and (back row) Mary Louise Bush, Elizabeth Ann Thompson, and Florence Simpson.

Camp Fire Girls pose for their photograph sometime in the 1950s. The nurse with the girls is probably Olga Espe Hanson, the superintendent of nursing at what was then Gritman Memorial Hospital (now Gritman Medical Center). The identities of the other two adults are unknown, as is the reason for the giggles the girls are just barely suppressing.

In 1954, attorney and insurance agent Laurence E. Huff published this map of Moscow. The University of Idaho Administration Building is identified on this one as well as the 1897 "Bird's Eye View of the City of Moscow, Latah County, Idaho" map of Moscow, but they are not the same building. The original administration building was destroyed by fire in 1906. Its replacement, completed in 1909, is still in use.

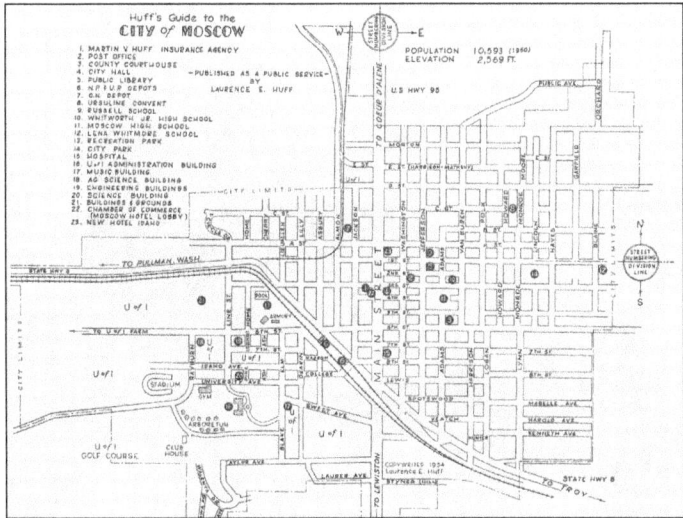

In the early 1930s, Mrs. Kelly's Boy's Singing Group pose for this photograph in the parlor of one of Moscow's premier residences, the McConnell Mansion, now a restored house and museum managed by the Latah County Historical Society. Pictured, from left to right , are Bobby Christenson, Bobby Smith, Frank Halverson, Harry Falkins, Billy Christenson, Gerry Hagedorn, and an unidentified boy.

Family portraiture in painting has existed for centuries, but the invention of photography in the 19th century made it affordable for the average family. This is a formal portrait of the John Almquist family in the 1880s. Mr. Almquist worked as a groundskeeper for the University of Idaho from its founding in 1890 to 1926. He died in 1927.

This later portrait of the John Almquist family probably dates to the mid- to late 1890s, when improvements in public health, sanitation, and diet, as well as reductions in infectious and parasitic diseases, began contributing significantly to a decline in infant and child mortality in the United States. Compare the two portraits of the Almquist family and see that all six children depicted in the earlier photograph can be found in this later one.

This is probably a portrait of the Charles Goetz family. With brother "Dutch Jake," Charles homesteaded in the Viola area of Latah County, roughly eight miles north of Moscow. Established in 1878 as Four Mile, Viola is one of the oldest communities in Latah County.

Harvest workers pose for their photograph on the Goetz homestead in northern Latah County. In the 1890s, the Goetz family grew wheat, oats, and barley. They also raised livestock, including cattle and hogs, and tended an orchard with apple, prune, walnut, and pear trees.

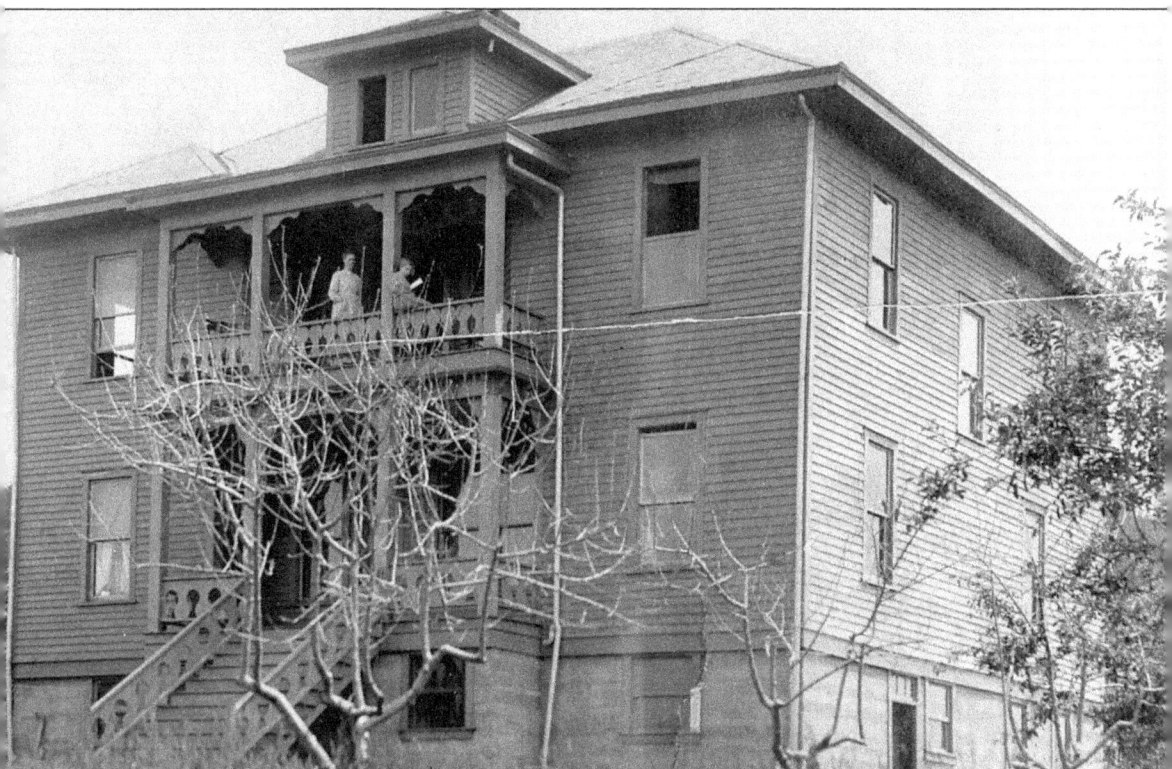

A young woman gazes from the balcony of the dormitory at Thatuna Intermediate School, a private boarding school owned and operated by the Seventh Day Adventists at Advent Hollow, two miles east of Viola. The boarding school closed in 1917, but day classes continued on the first floor of the dormitory until 1925.

This 1890s photograph was developed as a postcard and is noteworthy for the informality and spontaneity of its subjects. The inscription on the back reads, "J. Gilchrist, W. Taylor, Mrs. Criego and Mrs. Taylor at dinner in the wheat country near Moscow, Idaho."

Amateur photographer Roland Hodgins probably took this photograph of the Glen Sanders farm, one mile north of Moscow, around 1920. Moscow is located within the heart of the Palouse, one of the most productive agricultural regions in the world.

Five

POTLATCH

Potlatch's origins as a company town make it one of Latah County's most unique communities. In 1905, the Potlatch Lumber Company began construction on what was then the largest white pine sawmill in the world on a site in the northwestern part of Latah County. In addition to the mill, the company also built a town of homes, commercial buildings, schools, churches, a post office, and even an opera house. Nothing in this community was privately owned until the 1950s, when the company began selling its holdings in Potlatch, eventually closing the mill in 1981. For nearly 50 years, the Potlatch Lumber Company controlled not just the economic life of Potlatch but also its social and political lives.

In 1906, the population of Potlatch, which wasn't officially incorporated until 1952, was 1,000. Today not quite 800 people call Potlatch home.

Latah County's company town, Potlatch, had taken shape when this photograph was taken in April 1906. By the time the world's largest white pine sawmill began operating in September 1906, the Potlatch Lumber Company had constructed several hundred homes for families and a number of boardinghouses for single men.

This is the Mill that made our Reputation.

The Potlatch Mill, POTLATCH, Idaho.

Covering over 200 acres, the "mill that made our reputation" was also touted as the largest white pine sawmill in the world. William A. Wilkinson supervised construction of the mill, which began in the fall of 1905. A year later, on September 8, 1906, the first logs entered the mill.

William Deary, the general manager of the Potlatch Lumber Company when the Potlatch sawmill was built, poses for this photograph at the mill site. Born in Canada in the 1850s, Deary was an experienced logger and woodsman whom Potlatch historian Keith C. Petersen describes as "vigorous and visionary." He died in Potlatch in 1913.

Allison Laird, pictured here with wife Anna in 1911, was the first assistant general manager of the Potlatch Lumber Company. General manager William Deary "delegated to Laird much of the task of setting up the new community of Potlatch," according to Keith C. Petersen, the author of a history of Potlatch called *Company Town*.

Maxwell Williamson joined the Potlatch Lumber Company as an assistant sales manager in 1909. Outside the office, Williamson was a sports enthusiast who inspired the formation of the Potlatch Amateur Athletic Club.

According to *Company Town* author Keith C. Petersen, baseball was Potlatch's first organized sport, with a town team taking the field as early as 1907. Baseball was so popular in Potlatch that by 1913 there were four different town teams. This photograph, taken in 1912, is most likely one of those teams.

In its early years, Potlatch had many social and civic organizations, including a community band. Social gatherings were an important part of the Friday and Saturday nightlife of Potlatch. Holidays in particular offered special events, including a masquerade party on Halloween, a costume ball on St. Patrick's Day, and a barn dance on Thanksgiving. Independence Day was so special that the mill generally closed for the day.

Local performers provided much of the entertainment available in the early years of Potlatch. Schools offered programs regularly, and townspeople not only presented talent shows and plays but also organized community-wide banquets, such as the one in 1907 that celebrated the first anniversary of the mill's opening.

Like everything else in Potlatch, the schools were company-owned. The town's first school opened in 1906 and, the following year, the school moved into a new three-story building. Enrichment subjects, such as physical education, home economics, the manual arts, music, and art, were part of the curriculum from the beginning, and teachers were paid more than the state average.

This photograph of Potlatch's third grade in 1933–1934 reveals the ethnic diversity among the workforce of the lumber company. While the company preferred to hire men of American or northern European ancestry, it did occasionally hire men of other nationalities, including Greek, Italian, and Japanese. Predictably, the housing options of Greeks, Italians, and Japanese—even men with families—were limited to small cottages and boardinghouses.

Photographer Leo Oestreicher from Spokane, Washington, took this image of Potlatch's eighth-grade class in 1934–1935. From the late 1920s to about 1945, Oestreicher traveled the region photographing a variety of subjects, particularly school groups, sports, and other activities for school annuals.

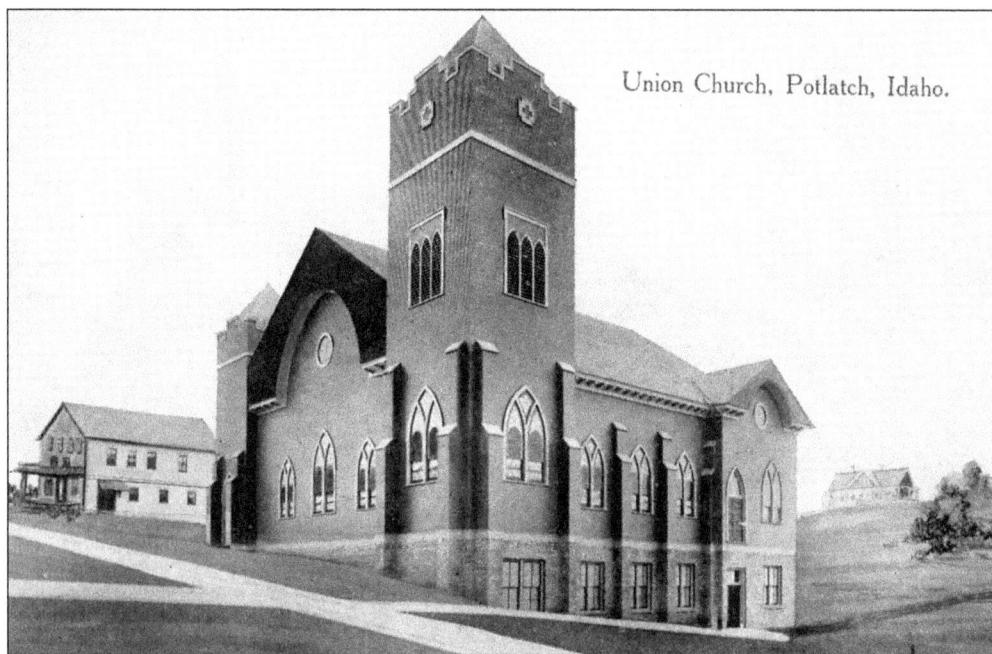

Union Church, Potlatch, Idaho.

The company managers believed a library was just as important to the community as were schools. Beginning in 1908 as a reading room, the first Potlatch library eventually evolved into the Potlatch Free Library that was housed initially in the Union Church. The Union Church, constructed in 1912, served over 20 Protestant denominations. The structure was destroyed by fire in 1951.

Window Display of One Thousand Pounds of Dwight Edwards Company's Steel Cut Chaffles Java and Mocha Coffee
POTLATCH MERCANTILE COMPANY. POTLATCH. IDAHO.

In 1907, A. A. McDonald was hired to manage the Potlatch Mercantile Company, known colloquially as the "Merc." With the goal of generating $1 million in sales annually, McDonald was an aggressive merchandiser who staged sales campaigns designed to reach consumers beyond the community of Potlatch.

The Potlatch Lumber Company provided housing for its employees, including several classes of family homes. The houses reserved for company management were steam-heated and rented for $40 a month. Pictured here is the home of general manager William Deary at 330 Cedar Street.

The streets of Potlatch were named for the deciduous trees the Potlatch Lumber Company planted in parks and along the streets: pine, locust, cedar, oak, elm, and maple. Locals still joke that the first letters of the street names stood for "Potlatch Lumber Company Owns Everything, Maybe." The identities of the people in this photograph, taken at the home located at 720 Cedar, are unknown.

Horses and other burden animals were once essential to logging operations. The horse barn on the Potlatch mill site, pictured here in 1908, was one of the largest in the region, with stall space for at least 100 horses. Often the teamsters were local men whose teams skidded logs during the times they weren't needed for plowing and harvest.

Near Potlatch, a group of loggers with their horses stop for the camera around 1895. Pictured, from left to right, are John Adair, Pete Clyde, "Grandpa" Adair, Bill Edmundson, and Bud Adair perched atop the log.

Largest Known White Pine Tree,
Felled December 12, 1911. Property of
Potlatch Lumber Company, POTLATCH, Idaho.
Copyright 1912 by G. B. Joslin.

The inscription on this photograph reads, "Largest Known White Pine Tree, Felled December 12, 1911. Property of Potlatch Lumber Company, POTLATCH, Idaho."

The Potlatch mill site contained two log ponds, and together they held nearly 20 million feet of logs. "Calk-booted log pond workers," explains Keith C. Petersen, "maneuvered logs to the bull chain, which transported them to the mill." Pictured in 1909, from left to right, are Henry Panky, unidentified, George Bird (seated), Charles Rambo, unidentified, Floyd Layton, and Harvey Shaffer.

Logs delivered to the mill by bull chains were cut to length by belt-driven chain saws. Sometimes referred to as "dentists," the saw filers who kept the miles of saws in condition were among the "most skilled and highly paid workers," according to Keith Petersen. Generally the saws had to be sharpened after each shift if not more often.

From the green chain, which conveyed newly-cut timber, lumber was then loaded into small railroad cars pulled by horses and transported to lumberyards where men unloaded and stacked the lumber. The stacks, often 20 feet high, were built with a slope to let water run off. This photograph, taken in 1913, may be of two stackers admiring their handiwork.

The men on the green-chain crew, one such team pictured here in 1909, pulled lumber off the chain and "slid it against their bodies before piling it on transfer cars," explains *Company Town* author Keith C. Petersen. Work on the green-chain crew was specialized, with each member handling one or several species and sizes of lumber.

The men pictured here are standing on stacks of finished lumber ready to be shipped from the mill by railroad cars. The loading dock at the mill could accommodate as many as 50 cars at one time, and the men who loaded the boards into the cars wore covers on their boots to keep the lumber clean.

Shipping crews were responsible for moving lumber from the mill to outside markets. Posing for this photograph, taken in 1914, is one such crew. Pictured, from left to right, are unidentified, Art Anderson, Basil Barker, unidentified, and Claude Stapleton.

Prior to 1918, when many of its workers left to join the country's World War I war efforts, the Potlatch Lumber Company hired women to work in the mill. The identities of these women workers in 1918 are unknown. Once the war ended and men returned to the mill, women workers were let go.

The Potlatch Lumber Company constructed its own railroad to haul logs and lumber. Completed in 1906, the Washington, Idaho & Montana Railway (WI&M) also carried passengers, agricultural products, livestock, and other items, such as the mail. The *Potlatcher*, built in 1937, was a WI&M car built specifically to deliver mail to communities along the line.

Photographer Leo Oestreicher, from Spokane, Washington, took this photograph of the fifth to eighth grades of Princeton's school in 1937–1938. Princeton, four miles east of Potlatch, was founded and named by lumberman Orville Clough in honor of his hometown of Princeton, Minnesota.

Civil War veteran Orpheus Jones moved to Deep Creek, several miles west of Potlatch and south of Freeze, in 1879. A Union soldier in the Iowa Infantry, Jones kept a journal of his experiences. The November 3, 1862, entry reads, "Brother tan Died at 3 oclock p m with Cold and measles and I war Detailed to Escort his body to the Depot for him to be Sent to his people."

Brothers Frank and Emery Herzog are pictured here around 1904. The Herzog family left Pennsylvania and settled in the Woodfell area of north central Latah County in 1901. Woodfell was a village north of Harvard in the Hoodoo Mining District. Emery died in 1945 and Frank in 1990.

Six

TROY

With homesteads dotting the ridges of grassland to its west and a dense white pine forest to the east, Troy was once a bustling trade and supply center. Fourteen miles east of Moscow, the community was known as Huffs Gulch when J. Wesley Seat homesteaded in the area in 1885. In 1890, area businessman John P. Vollmer immodestly changed the name of the town to his surname when he brought in the railroad. In 1897, citizens decided to rename the town in an act of rebellion against the very unpopular Vollmer, who then owned over 30,000 acres of land, much of it gained through foreclosing on the bank loans of local farmers. According to legend, the name of "Troy" was suggested by a Greek railroad worker and selected as a result of the shots of whiskey the man offered to anyone who would vote to change the name. In 1908, the population of Troy was 700. Today it is a little less than 800.

This photograph of what is now Troy was taken sometime in the 1890s, probably before 1898 when the town's first brick building was constructed. Troy grew rapidly in the 1890s and, by 1894, had four churches, two newspapers, and a school.

Large numbers of Scandinavians settled in the Troy area during the 1880s and 1890s. Many were persuaded to move to Idaho by people already settled in the area, such as native Swede Per Johanson (third from left in the fur coat). For many, the move was from the American Midwest, not directly from one of the Scandinavian countries. The other men in the c. 1908 photograph, from left to right, are Lars Hegstrom, John Carmen, and Bob Olson.

Emil Fredman, age 19 when this photograph was taken, left Sweden in 1887 to homestead with brothers Carl and Albert on Dry Ridge, northeast of Troy. Emil and his wife Augusta, also a native of Sweden, had six children, all girls.

Nestled within a forest so thick that "birds could scarcely fly through," according to a 1903 history of northern Idaho, sawmills were one of the first commercial activities in the area of Troy. Hank Skeel's sawmill, built in the mid-1880s, was located near Troy on American Ridge.

A native of Norway, O. K. Olson moved to Troy from Iowa in 1902. He became a logger and operated a sawmill for many years. The identities of the men in this photograph, taken at Olson's mill, are unknown, but the author wonders if the man standing might not be O. K. Olson himself.

The Hotel Reitmann, built by Charles Reitmann in 1898, was the first brick structure in Troy. Promoting itself as the "biggest little town on earth" by the early 1900s, Troy offered area residents a brisk commercial center complete with a bank, four general stores, a flour mill, two meat markets, and three saloons. The Hotel Reitmann is on the National Register of Historic Places.

John P. Vollmer, a native of Germany, changed the name of the village of Huffs Gulch to Vollmer in 1890 after he extended a line of the Spokane and Palouse Railway to the community. In some circles, he was known as the shrewdest businessman in Idaho, and in others he was its most aggressive. In addition to Troy, Vollmer also had business interests in other Latah County towns, including Genesee.

The men in this photograph are identified as the "Business Men of Troy, 1904." By 1919, Troy was the one of the most important shipping points in the entire Inland Northwest, with hundreds of railcar loads of railroad ties, wood, grain, hay, and beans being shipped to outside markets.

Troy's Main Street is pictured here as it appeared on Fair Day in 1920. The business of Jack Pickerd was located in the lower section of the Hotel Troy, seen in the left background. A 1924 newspaper advertisement for Pickerd states, "Licensed Embalmer and Undertaker," and informs potential customers that during "bad weather we will furnish horse drawn hearse."

Next to the Pickerd funeral home was the Modernistic Beauty Shoppe that was owned by Erma Shultz Harland, who is pictured here with Opal Dragstead. In 1934, Erma moved to Troy from Potlatch, where she had worked for the Potlatch Company Beauty Shop. Erma married Maurice Harland on February 2, 1942.

Per Johanson, an early Troy area settler, organized the Idaho Fire Brick and Clay Company in 1912 on a 15-acre site on the western edge of Troy. The identities of the brick workers pictured in this 1917 photograph are unknown, but the author wonders if the man in shirt and vest at right might not be J. B. Watson, who managed the plant from 1917 to 1928.

Maurice Harland was the son of Manford and Emma Harland, who homesteaded on American Ridge south of Troy. This photograph of the Harland children was taken in 1913. Pictured clockwise, from left to right, are Maurice, Millard, Grace, Raymond, Josephine (on Faith's lap), Faith, Dorsey (standing), and Ada.

Near American Ridge and about two miles southwest of Troy is Driscoll Ridge, named for the ridge's first homesteaders. In 1892, Joseph Driscoll married Moscow schoolteacher Elizabeth McGarr. This photograph was taken on their wedding day. Joseph died in 1937 and Elizabeth in 1957.

In 1878, George Driscoll, his brother-in-law Patrick Cunningham, and his father, John, left New Brunswick, Canada, to homestead in what would be known as the Driscoll Ridge area of Latah County, near Troy. This photograph of the Patrick and Mary Cunningham family was taken in 1894. Pictured, from left to right, are (first row) Mayme, Patrick, Catherine, Mary, and Elizabeth; (second row) William, Margaret, John, Isabelle, and Nellie.

106

The families of Harmer Chaney and Martha Sly arrived in Latah County, near American Ridge, in 1883. Harmer, 24, and Martha, 16, are pictured here on their wedding day on October 24, 1888. Martha died in 1947 and Harmer in 1954.

Nora, a small trading center, was established about five miles northeast of Troy in 1892. One of the families to settle in the Pleasant Hill area near Nora was that of Aaron and Mary Johnson. Natives of Sweden, Aaron and Mary pose in this photograph, taken in 1909, with their children at the family home. Pictured, from left to right, are (first row) Ethel, Aaron, Walter, and Mary; (second row) Clarence, William, Alvin, Hilma, and Elmer.

Cornwall was an early Latah County community located on the Northern Pacific Railroad line between Moscow and Troy. Originally known as Bronta Cabin and Otto, the village was named for Mason Cornwall, a successful Latah County businessman and landowner. The extended family of George and Lucinda Walker, pictured here in the 1890s, lived in the Cornwall area.

Joel was an early Latah County community located on the Northern Pacific Railroad line between Moscow and Troy. Moscow businessman William Kaufmann agreed to donate land to the railroad for a depot at what became Joel if the railroad agreed to name the station after his son Joel. According to the inscription on this 1890s photograph of David and Sara Lee, the couple operated a livery stable and boardinghouse in Joel.

A native of Norway, Simon Johnson married Lela Kerns Bailey on December 24, 1902. Simon and Lela left Orofino, Idaho, in 1910 to settle in the Big Meadow area of Latah County, near Troy. Their daughter Stella married Elmer Johnson, the son of Aaron and Mary Johnson. Stella would go on to write A *History of Troy*, published in 1992.

Hay harvest on Little Bear Ridge is interrupted for this 1890s photograph. A pulley-controlled fork, which was operated by ropes, supports the hay suspended in the air. It appears that the gentleman on top of the hay pile in the wagon is holding a rope, and if he were to tug on it he would release the load onto the neighboring stack.

The people in this 1890s photograph, taken in the Joel/Cornwall area, are most likely members of a threshing crew. Threshing was a labor, equipment, and time-intensive part of harvest. No single farmer could afford to own his own threshing outfit, so he generally hired a contract thresher who moved his equipment and crew from farmstead to farmstead.

Public education in the Troy area dates back to 1893 when the Pioneer School was built on what was then Vollmer's Main Street. Professor Smith, Nellie Edwin, Norma Taylor, and Mary Cole are identified as Troy's teachers in 1906.

MONTHLY REPORT
of

Lawrence Rambo

Grade 2nd

Oct 2d   19 2_

Pleasant Hills   School

Studies, Etc.	1st Mo	2d Mo	3rd Mo	4th Mo	5th Mo	6th Mo	7th Mo	8th Mo	9th Mo	Term Avg.
Reading	81	82	82	85						
Spelling	80	82	86	82						
Writing	82	83	84	89						
Drawing	82	83	84	85						
Arithmetic	80	82	83	86						
Grammar										
Geography										
History										
Physiology										
Civil Govt										
Lang	81	82	83	89						
Deportment	84	84	84	84						
Days Absent	1	0	0	1						
Times Tardy	1	0	2	1						

1. 100, 10, or P is Perfect; 90, 9, or E. is Excellent; 80, 8, or G. is Good; 70, 7, or F. is Fair; 60, 6. or U. is Unsatisfactory.

2. Low mark in deportment generally means wasted time and hindrance to others.

3. Please give careful consideration to anything underscored.

Lena _____ Troy _____ Teacher.

At one time, there was more than one Pleasant Hill School in Latah County. The one Laurence Rambo attended in 1908 was located on Nora Creek, about four miles northeast of Troy. Sadly Laurence's life was short. He was born on May 27, 1902, and died on November 20, 1918. The inscription on his headstone reads, "Gone in life's bright morn! Gone in his youthful bloom!"

112

This advertisement for the Idaho Fire Brick Company was published in the yearbook of the Troy High School class of 1927. In his editorial, editor Glenn C. Todd explains that the senior class chose for their motto, "Don't Be a Crank, Be a Self-Starter" because "our class has always been an original class."

Blanche Rambo, at left, was the daughter of William and Olive Rambo and sister of Laurence Rambo. She is pictured here in 1910 as a student nurse, training with "head nurse" Mrs. Smith at Moscow's Gritman Hospital. The apron Blanche wears in the photograph is in the garment collection of the Latah County Historical Society.

Longtime Troy area resident James Lange, or "Uncle Jimmy," is pictured here celebrating his 100th birthday on January 22, 1934. Lange died later that year. The cake, topped with 100 candles, was a gift from members of the Troy Grange No. 280, founded in 1931.

Spokane photographer Leo Oestreicher took this image of the Troy High School girls' basketball team sometime in the early to mid-1930s. From the late 1920s to about 1945, Oestreicher traveled the region photographing a variety of subjects, particularly school groups, sports, and other activities for school annuals.

Among the 13 students graduating from Troy High School on May 14, 1945, were Lloyd Torell, at left, and Howard Dyer, pictured here in full football regalia.

The 1933–1934 students of Troy High School strike an original pose for photographer Leo Oestreicher of Spokane, Washington. Many of Oestreicher's black-and-white images were made into lithographed postcards and sold as souvenirs.

Seven

THE UNIVERSITY OF IDAHO

The University of Idaho was founded on January 30, 1889, when the governor of the Idaho Territory signed Council Bill 20, cowritten by Latah County residents John Brigham and Willis Sweet. Sweet, as first president and secretary of the board of regents, along with Moscow physician Henry Blake, purchased a 20-acre tract of land from James Deakin, one of Moscow's largest landowners. While excavation of the site, a hill to the southwest of downtown Moscow, began in 1889, construction did not begin until 1891.

On October 3, 1892, Pres. Franklin B. Gault officially opened the university when he welcomed several dozen students and one professor, John Edwin Ostrander. Current student population at the university now exceeds 12,000.

SEMI-CENTENNIAL

THE OLD ADMINISTRATION BUILDING DESTROYED BY FIRE IN 1906

UNIVERSITY OF IDAHO
1889-1939

ANNIVERSARY DINNER
Sunday, January 29, 1939

HOTEL MOSCOW—MENU

SOUVENIR MENU
Sunday, January 29, 1939

DINNER

CONSOMME A LA ROYAL
OR CREAM OF CHICKEN SOUP
ASSORTED PICKLES AND OLIVES

CRAB A LA NEWBURG   RELISH

CHOICE OF
FRENCH LAMB CHOPS ON TOAST   75c
T-BONE STEAK, LONG BRANCH POTATOES   85c
NEW YORK CUT SIRLOIN STEAK   75c
FRIED EASTERN OYSTERS, LEMON   75c
FRIED YOUNG CHICKEN AND GRAVY   75c
CREAMED CHICKEN PATTIES   60c
BAKED VIRGINIA HAM, ORANGE SAUCE   60c
PRIME RIB OF BEEF AU JUS   60c
ROAST STUFFED CHICKEN, CELERY DRESSING   75c

BAKED IDAHO POTATO   ESCALLOPED CORN
OR SWEET POTATO, SOUTHERN
MOSCOW HOUSE ROLLS

MACEDOINE FRUITS SALAD

DESSERTS
APPLE PIE AND CHEESE   CHERRY PIE   MINCE PIE
WASHINGTON CREAM PIE
VANILLA, CHOCOLATE OR STRAWBERRY ICE CREAM
WITH LAYER CAKE
FRUIT PARFAIT   CHARLOTTE RUSSE
CAFE NOIR   CAFE AU LAIT

Reflecting the close ties between "town and gown," the semi-centennial of the University of Idaho was celebrated by Moscow's premier hotel with an anniversary dinner on Sunday, January 29, 1939. Elsie Nelson, born on a farmstead just outside Moscow to Swedish parents, most likely selected the celebratory menu as supervisor of the food operations at Hotel Moscow.

John Warren Brigham of Genesee was a Latah County representative to the Idaho territorial legislature. He introduced legislation written with Willis Sweet to establish the University of Idaho in Moscow. On January 30, 1889, Gov. Edward Stevenson signed the act into law in Brigham's presence.

Charles R. Stillinger, right, was born in 1889, the same year the University of Idaho was created. He would go on to earn his bachelor's and master's degrees from the university and become one of its most generous financial supporters. At left is Charles's brother Otto, and the gentleman between the two World War I soldiers is J. C. Stillinger, the father of the two men. This *c.* 1918 photograph was taken at the Stillinger home south of Moscow.

"Idaho Violet Rosch Ormsby," the university's purebred Jersey cow, pictured at the end of the table in the background, is honored with a banquet in 1923 despite her reputation for being wild-eyed, flighty, and given to chase at the slightest annoyance.

A research team from the University of Idaho and Utah State University was the first to clone a member of the horse family—a mule. Idaho Gem, born on May 4, 2003, is at right with handler Jessica Williams. Two other mule clones, Utah Pioneer (middle) and Idaho Star (left) were born later in the year. (University of Idaho, Kelly Weaver, Copyright 2004.)

UNIVERSITY OF IDAHO

Jas. A. MacLean, Ph. D., LL. D., Pres.

This University was founded at Moscow in 1892. Although one of the country's youngest institutions the Carnegie trustees, after making an exhaustive investigation of university ratings, placed the U. of I in the front rank.

Armory and Gymnasium

The new Administration building now being erected at a cost of $300,000, will have a ground space of 274 x 130 feet and will be ready for occupancy in September, 1909.

Morrill Hall, Agriculture

Ridenbaugh Hall, the Girls' Dormitory

The University of Idaho comprises:
I. The College of Letters and Sciences.
II. The College of Agriculture.
III. The Idaho Agricultural Experiment Station.

The Engineering Building

IV. The College of Engineering, civil, mining, electrical and mechanical.

The Mill —Mining

V. The School of Law.
VI. The Preparatory School.

The College affords courses in Domestic Economy, Music, Elocution, Physical Education, Literary Science, Military Science and Tactics and short courses in Dairying and Forestry.

Assay Building

This postcard shows off the impressive buildings on the University of Idaho campus in 1910. Ridenbaugh Hall, which now houses music and art programs, was first occupied in 1902 as a women's dormitory. It was named in honor of Mary E. Ridenbaugh, the then vice president of the university's board of regents. Constructed in 1906 to house the College of Agriculture and the Agricultural Experiment Station, Morrill Hall also remains in use today.

In 1929, students Malcolm Renfrew, at left, and Gerald Ingle indulge in some horseplay, striking the perfect poses for the ice-covered sidewalk outside University of Idaho dormitory Lindley Hall. Renfrew would go on to be a professor of chemistry at the university, making major contributions to the field of polymer chemistry. Ingle, who was born on his parent's farm on Big Bear Ridge, would remain in Latah County all of his life, working as a farmer and once serving as a Latah County commissioner.

For many years, the Blue Bucket Orchestra was the hottest jazz band in Moscow. This orchestra, pictured c. 1932, included William Hawkins and Glenn Exum, third and fourth from the left.

The Blue Bucket Chorus Line performs along side the Blue Bucket Orchestra around 1932. The Blue Bucket was the university's first student center. The name is an allusion to Idaho's mining history. Prospectors were said to have struck it rich when they had enough gold nuggets to fill a blue bucket.

During World War II, the University of Idaho hosted the Naval Radio Training School. Between May 15, 1942, and January 15, 1945, the United States Navy instructed nearly 4,500 people on how to receive and send code at what was one of the most celebrated training programs in the nation. This class of operators graduated in 1945.

During the 1950–1951 school year, with the nation embroiled in the Korean Conflict, thousands of University of Idaho students participated in what is believed to have been the first campus-wide blood drive. The very successful effort drew the attention of the national media, with pieces in *Life* magazine and on the radio programs of Drew Pearson and Walter Winchell.

Positioned at the windows of the upper floors of Upham Hall, a men's dormitory on the University of Idaho campus, upperclassmen "welcome" freshmen hall mates by dumping buckets of water on their heads as they pose for a group photograph. The image is courtesy of brothers Bill and Chick Mabbutt, residents still of Latah County. Bill is fourth from the left in the front row, and his brother Chick is fifth from the left.

In 1931, Mi and Marie Lew, natives of China, were married in Moscow. They made their home there until Mi's death in 1982 and Marie's in 1984. Stressing the importance of education, the couple saw their five children—Claire, Merry, Sheryl, Gary, and Dennis—all graduate from the University of Idaho.

BIBLIOGRAPHY

Boone, Lalia Phipps. *From A to Z in Latah County, Idaho: A Place Name Dictionary*. Idaho Place Name Project, 1983.

Driscoll, Ann Nilsson. *They Came to a Ridge*. Moscow, ID: The News Review Publishing Company, 1970.

Harris, R. K. "Life in Potlatch Was Different." *The Pacific Northwesterner*. Volume 20, Number 1, Winter 1976.

Idahonian. Moscow, Latah County, and University of Idaho Centennial Editions.

Johnson, Stella E. *History of Troy*. Troy, ID: Self-published, 1992.

A Centennial History of the Kendrick-Juliaetta Area. Kendrick, ID: Kendrick-Juliaetta Centennial Committee, 1990.

Monroe, Julie R. *Moscow, Idaho: Living and Learning on the Palouse*. Charleston, SC: Arcadia Publishing, 2003.

Nelson, Elsie Mary. *Today is Ours*. Self-published, 1972.

Otness, Lillian W. *A Great Good Country*. Moscow, ID: Latah County Historical Society, 1983.

Petersen, Keith C. *Company Town: Potlatch, Idaho and the Potlatch Lumber Company*. Pullman, WA: Washington State University Press, 1987.

Petersen, Keith and Richard Waldbauer. *Troy, Deary and Genesee: A Photographic History*. Moscow, ID: Latah County Historical Society, 1979.

Waldbauer, Richard C. *Grubstaking the Palouse: Gold Mining in the Hoodoo Mountains of North Idaho, 1860–1950*. Pullman, WA: Washington State University Press, 1986.

Additional resources from the archives of Latah County Historical Society include archival documents and articles from the *Latah Legacy*, authored by Thomas Femreite, Carolyn Gravelle, Rosemary Huskey, John B. Miller, Robbin T. Johnston, Agnes Healy Jones, Ray E. Osterberg, Keith C. Petersen, Mary E. Reed, Marie Scharnhorst, and Herman C. Schufer.

Visit us at
arcadiapublishing.com

www.ingramcontent.com/pod-product-compliance
Lightning Source LLC
Chambersburg PA
CBHW050646110426
42813CB00007B/1932